Zaner-Bloser

HANDWRITING

BASIC SKILLS and APPLICATION
Revised Edition

Book 2 Manuscript

WALTER B. BARBE, Ph.D.

Editor-in-Chief, *Highlights for Children*;
Adjunct Professor, The Ohio State University

VIRGINIA H. LUCAS, Ph.D.

Professor of Education,
Wittenberg University, Springfield, Ohio

THOMAS M. WASYLYK

Master Penman and Handwriting Specialist;
Past President, International Association of Master Penmen,
Engrossers, and Teachers of Handwriting

CLINTON S. HACKNEY

Master Penman and Professional Handwriting Consultant,
Tampa, Florida

LOIS A. BRAUN

Supervisor, Elementary Curriculum,
Santa Monica-Malibu (California) Unified School District

The Sam Houston Schoolhouse at Maryville, Tennessee. In 1812 Sam Houston taught here. Students ranged in age from 6 to 60 and paid their tuition in corn, calico, and cash. Sam Houston went on to become Governor of Tennessee and, later, Governor of Texas.

D1510898

Zaner-Bloser, Inc., Columbus, Ohio

Copyright © 1987, Zaner-Bloser, Inc.

Zaner-Bloser, Inc., P.O. Box 16764, Columbus, Ohio 43216-6764

Printed in the United States of America

Years ago, many schoolhouses were one-room log cabins. Students of all ages were taught by one teacher in the same room.

Write the sentences. Use your best writing.

CHECK-UP

	CORRECT	INCORRECT
letter formation	☐	☐
vertical quality	☐	☐
spacing	☐	☐
alignment and proportion	☐	☐
line quality	☐	☐

My Alphabet _____

Write the **lower-case** manuscript letter for each letter below.

A _ B _ C _ D _ E _

F _ G _ H _ I _ J _ K _

L _ M _ N _ O _ P _

Q _ R _ S _ T _ U _

V _ W _ X _ Y _ Z _

PAPER POSITION _____

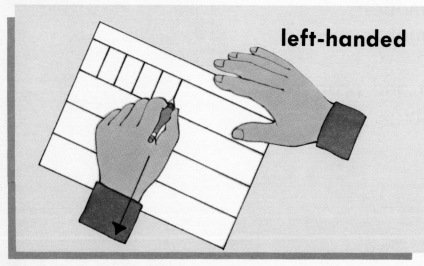

left-handed

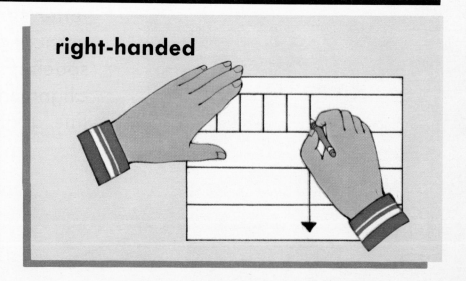

right-handed

Write the **upper-case** manuscript letter for each letter below.

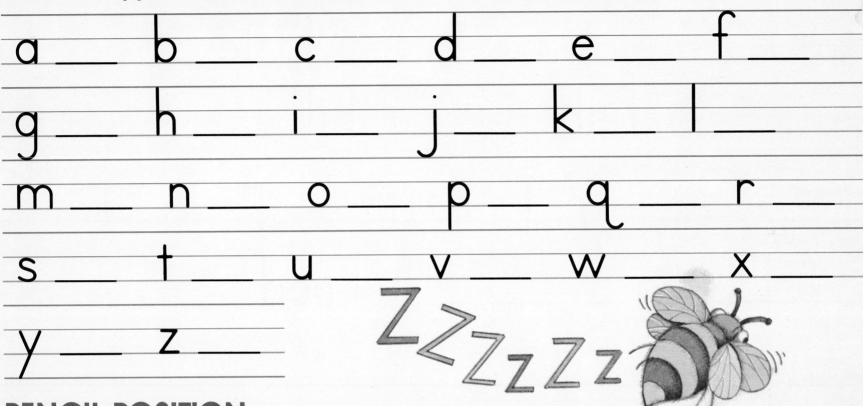

a___ b___ c___ d___ e___ f___

g___ h___ i___ j___ k___ l___

m___ n___ o___ p___ q___ r___

s___ t___ u___ v___ w___ x___

y___ z___

PENCIL POSITION

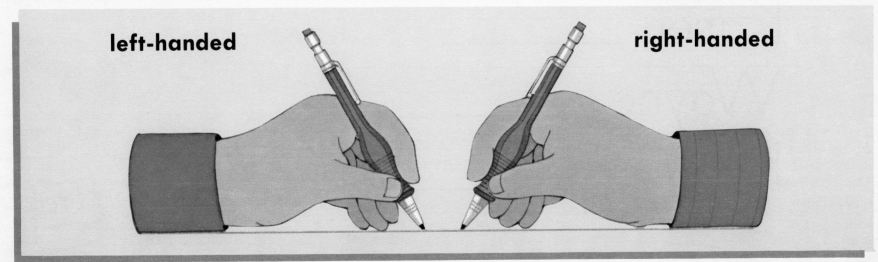

left-handed   right-handed

Basic Strokes

Trace and write the basic strokes. Write the letters and words.

l l ___ l l ___ little ___

fish ___ hill ___

L E F T

Elvira ___ Fred ___

/ / ___ / / ___

Karen ___

Wayne ___

Kim ___

wavy

toad   dog

bubbles

Write the sentence.

I have a pet puppy.

My Writing Lines

1. headline → _____
2. midline → _____
3. baseline → _____

Write the name of each writing line.

_____ _____ _____

1. _____ 2. _____ 3. _____

SIZE OF LETTERS

bhB   t   aem   gy

tall letters **middle-size letter** **short letters** **tail letters**

Circle the tail letters in the sentence.

The dog can jump quickly.

Write eight short letters. _____

Write six tall letters. _____

8

Write the word that has a middle-size letter in it.

look   car   tree   bell

Write four tail letters.

ALIGNMENT

All letters rest on the baseline. Write the word.

bread

Short letters touch the midline. Write the word.

moon

Tall letters touch the headline. Write the word.

Bubble

Tail letters fill the space below the baseline. Write the word.

puppy

My alignment is:

CORRECT ☐

INCORRECT ☐

Numerals

Trace and write the numerals.

1 1 _____ _____ _____

2 2 _____ _____ _____

3 3 _____ _____ _____

4 4 _____ _____ _____

5 5 _____ _____ _____

6 6 _____ _____ _____

7 7 _____ _____ _____

8 8 _____ _____ _____

9 9 _____ _____ _____

10 10 _____ _____ _____

Write the number words.

1 one

2 two

3 three

4 four

5 five

6 six

7 seven

8 eight

9 nine

10 ten

PAPER POSITION

left-handed

right-handed

Vertical Quality

little
CORRECT

little
INCORRECT

Write the sentence two times.

Hank kicked the football.

PENCIL POSITION

left-handed   **right-handed**

Line Quality

hold
CORRECT

hold
INCORRECT

Write the sentence two times.

The turtle won the race.

 My line quality is good.   **YES** ☐   **NO** ☐

Spacing

...BETWEEN LETTERS

vertical lines	**vertical lines and circles**	**two circles**
all	lion	book
most space	slightly less space	least amount of space

Write the name of each animal.

frog _____ _____

monkey _____ _____

moose _____ _____

gorilla _____ _____

CHECK-UP

	CORRECT	**INCORRECT**
My spacing between letters is:	☐	☐

14

...BETWEEN WORDS

One lower-case **o** should fit between words.

This●is●correct●spacing.

Write this sentence. Check your spacing between words.

I can write well.

...BETWEEN SENTENCES

Two lower-case **o**'s should fit between sentences.
Write the sentences two times.

See the red cart!●●It is mine.

SALAD DELIGHT

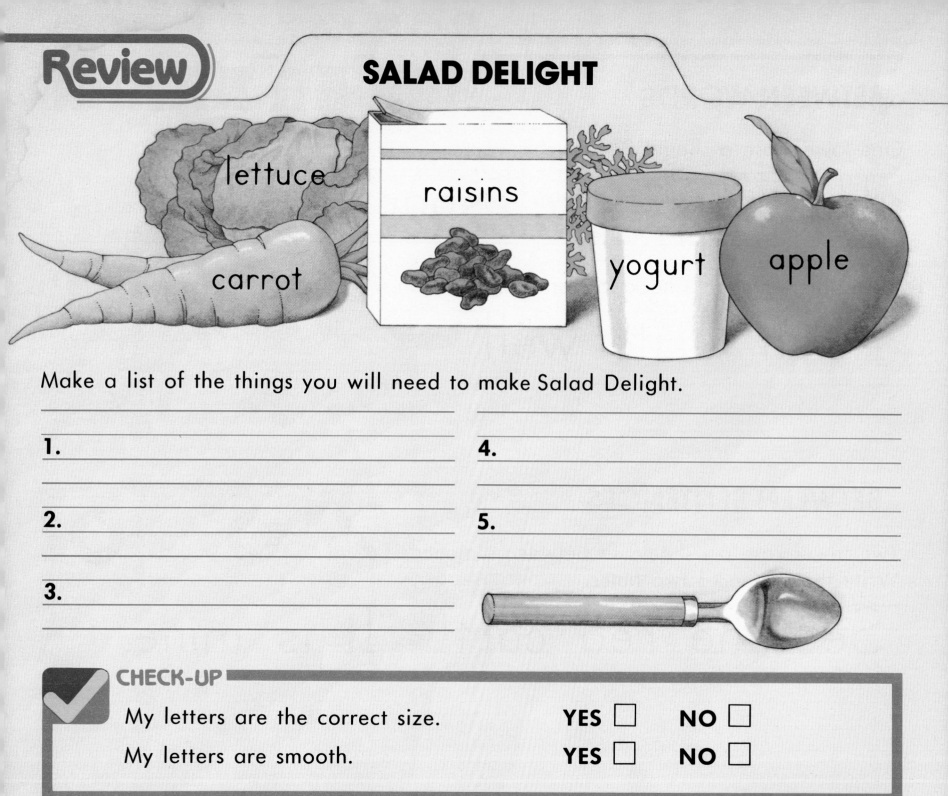

lettuce

raisins

carrot

yogurt

apple

Make a list of the things you will need to make Salad Delight.

1. _____

2. _____

3. _____

4. _____

5. _____

CHECK-UP

My letters are the correct size.   YES ☐   NO ☐

My letters are smooth.   YES ☐   NO ☐

DIRECTIONS

Cut a small carrot and half an apple into pieces.
Put into a bowl. Add raisins and two tablespoons
of yogurt. Mix. Serve on a lettuce leaf.

Write the directions.

_____

_____

_____

_____

_____

_____

_____

_____

_____

_____

_____

_____

_____

_____

Trace and write the letters.

Write the words.

Luis _____   little _____

Irene _____   flying _____

Write the sentence.

Lee and I like to ride bikes.

People Travel in Different Ways

Write the sentences.

Ida sails the sea in a ship.

Luis is the pilot of a plane.

Write these ways to travel.

1. plane

2. ship

3. balloon

1. _____

2. _____

3. _____

How would you like to travel?

_____

_____

Trace and write the letters.

t T

Write the words.

trees

dirt

root

pretty

trunk

later

Write the sentence.

Trees need water to grow.

PAPER POSITION

left-handed

right-handed

Write the sentence.

Tall trees grow from tiny seeds.

A trunk, a limb, a leaf, and roots are parts of a tree.

Write the parts of this tree.

Trace and write the letters.

o o o

O O O

a a a

A A A

Write the words.

Ollie

onion

Amy

away

Write the sentence.

Angela picks apples in October.

oranges

apples

pears

o
O
a
A

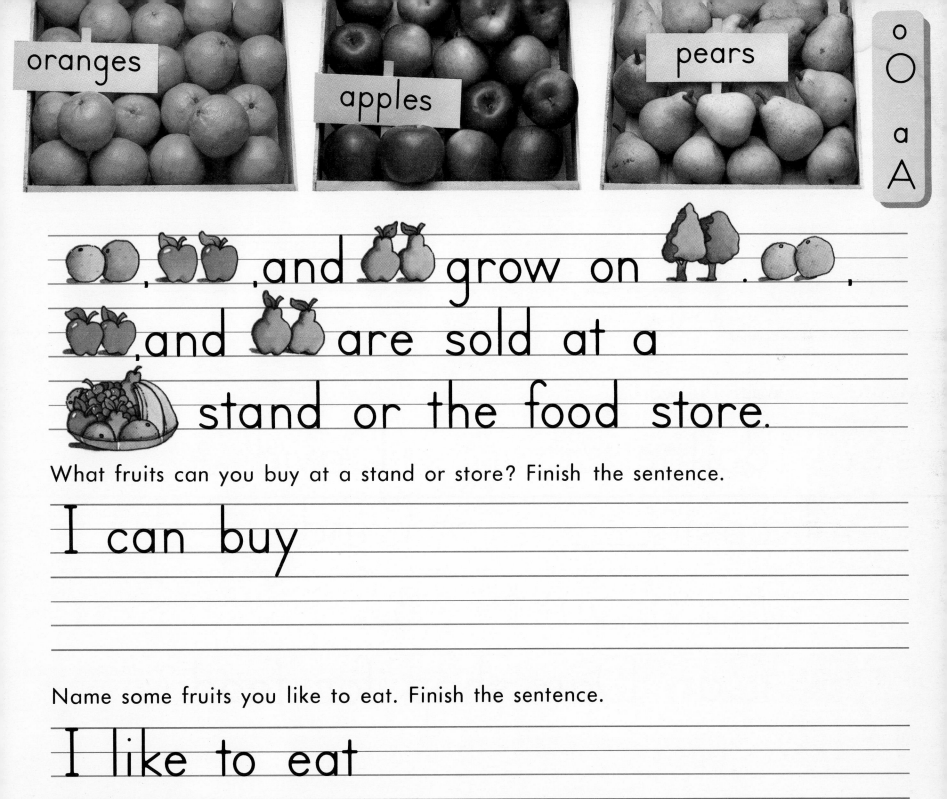

🍊🍊 , 🍎🍎 ,and 🍐🍐 grow on 🌳🌳 . 🍊🍊 , 🍎🍎 ,and 🍐🍐 are sold at a 🧺 stand or the food store.

What fruits can you buy at a stand or store? Finish the sentence.

I can buy

Name some fruits you like to eat. Finish the sentence.

I like to eat

23

Trace and write the letters.

d D   d   d   d

D   D   D   D

c C   c   c   c

        C   C   C

Write the words.

dollar _____   David _____

cost _____   Cindy _____

Write the question.

?   Can Dan shop for food?

Neighborhood Stores _____

You asked a friend to come for lunch.
You must go to the store for some food.
You pass other stores on
your way. Look at the path
you will take.

Write the name of the first store you will pass.

_____

1. _____

You stop at the next store for some rolls. Write its name.

_____

2. _____

It is fun to look inside the third store. Write its name.

_____

3. _____

Write the name of the store where you will shop.

_____

4. _____

Drug Store

Pet Land

City Bakery

Food Town

1 2 3 4

25

Trace and write each letter.

e e e _ _ _ _ _ _ _ e

E E E _ _ _ _ _ _ _ E

f f f _ _ _ _ _ _ _ f

F F F _ _ _ _ _ _ _ F

Write the words.

elf _____ Eric _____

fifth _____ Felice _____

Write the sentence.

I can write e, E, f, and F.

Write these words on the sign:
Fresh Fish

We like to eat fresh fish.

Draw fish on this sign.

e E f F.

Look at the picture. Write a sentence telling who likes to eat fresh fish.

_____

_____

_____

_____

What do you like to eat?

_____

_____

_____

Write eight words using the letters below.

l L   i I   t T   o O   a A

d D   c C   e E   f F

1. _____

2. _____

3. _____

4. _____

5. _____

6. _____

7. _____

8. _____

What other words can you write?

28

Write a story. Use as many words
from page 28 as you can.

CHECK-UP

	YES	NO
My spacing is correct.	☐	☐
My letters are the correct size.	☐	☐
My line quality is correct.	☐	☐
My letter forms are correct.	☐	☐

Trace and write the letters.

Write the words.

goldfish _____

jungle _____

Greg _____

Jill _____

Write the sentence.

Joan gave Gus a jar of guppies.

Ginger owns a horse. Ginger's horse gallops and jumps when she rides it.

Juan has goldfish and jewelfish. Juan keeps the goldfish in a bowl and the jewelfish in a tank.

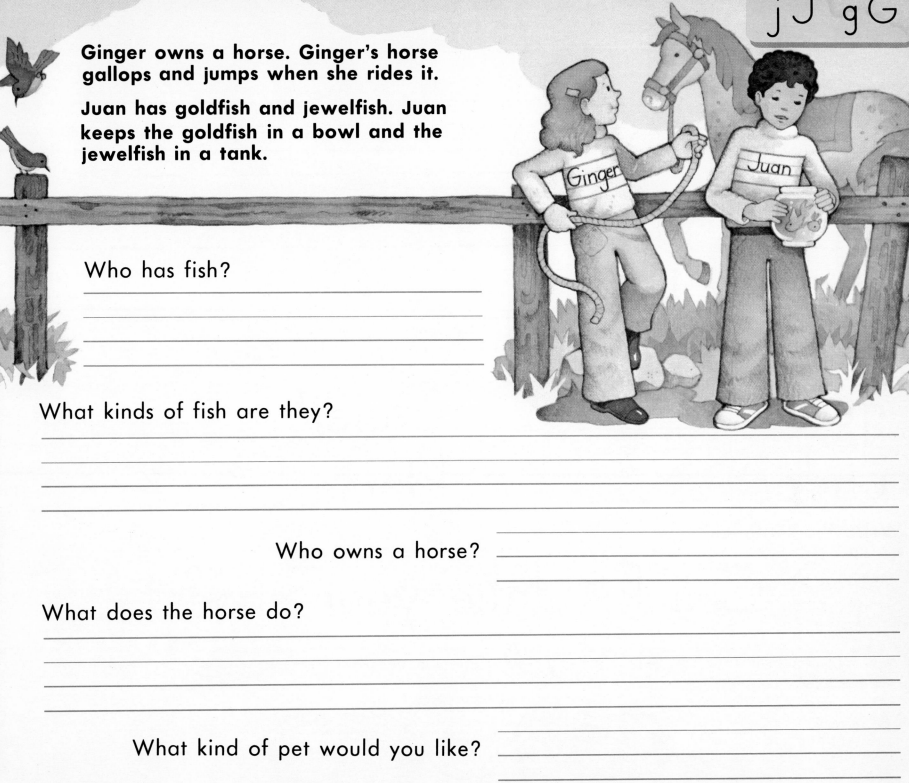

Who has fish?

_____

_____

_____

What kinds of fish are they?

_____

_____

_____

Who owns a horse? _____

_____

What does the horse do?

_____

_____

_____

What kind of pet would you like? _____

_____

Trace and write the letters.

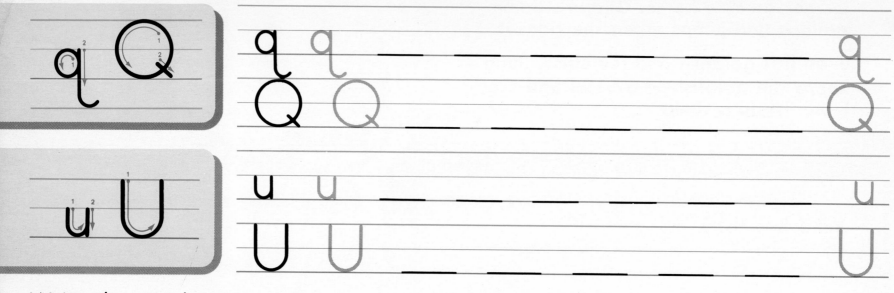

Write the words.

quart

Quiet!

under

Uncle

Write the sentence.

!

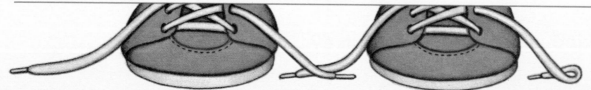

Quick! Untie your shoes!

qQ uU !

Write the missing letters. Use **Q**, **o**, **u**, **i**, or **e**.

B_g as a h__s_!

St_bborn as a m__l!

_u_ck as a w_nk!

Co_l as a c_c_mb_r!

_uiet as a m__s_!

Finish these phrases with your own words.

Quiet as

Quick as

33

Trace and write the letters.

s S   s s _ _ _ _ _ s

S S _ _ _ _ _ S

Write each word.

sister _____   stairs _____

Sally _____   Steven _____

This•is•correct•spacing.

Write the sentence. Space your words correctly.

Susan uses scissors safely.

Write the title **Safety at School**.

Stop at the sign.
Walk in the halls.

STOP

Swing and slide safely.
Stand in line.

Write the sentences about safety.

My spacing is correct.   **YES** ☐   **NO** ☐

Write the lower-case letter for each letter below.

G _____ J _____ Q _____ U _____ S _____

Write the upper-case letter for each letter below.

s _____ u _____ q _____ j _____ g _____

1. _____

How many things can you find in this picture that begin with the letter **s**? Write the words.

2. _____

3. _____

4. _____

5. _____

6. _____

Spacing

This sentence is hard to read. Why?

Aprilshowersbring Mayflowers.

Write the sentence with correct spacing.

_____

_____

_____

_____

Write why you think correct spacing is important.

_____

_____

_____

_____

Write three things you see in spring.

_____

1. _____

2. _____

3. _____

My letters are spaced correctly.
YES ☐   **NO** ☐

My words are spaced correctly.
YES ☐   **NO** ☐

Trace and write the letters.

b b _____ b

B B _____ B

h h _____ h

H H _____ H

" "

Write the sentences.

Barb said, "Hal won the race."

"Here we are," said Belinda.

Good Teeth for a Happy Smile

Brush your teeth after meals. Have your teeth checked by your dentist.

Write what the dentist says about your teeth.

The dentist says,

CHECK-UP

Did you put quotation marks around the sentences the dentist says?

YES ☐ NO ☐

39

Trace and write the letters.

p P   p   p   p

P   P   P   P

r R   r   r   r

R   R   R   R

Write the words.

purple _____

rope _____

Patricia _____

Ralph _____

40

Planning a Trip

Write the paragraph about Pat and Ralph's trip.

Pat, Ralph, and their family plan a picnic in the country. They will row a boat. They will fish in the river. They will leave the area clean.

Trace and write the letters.

n n n ___ ___ ___ ___ ___ ___ ___ ___ n

N N N ___ ___ ___ ___ ___ ___ ___ ___ N

m m m ___ ___ ___ ___ ___ ___ ___ m

M M M ___ ___ ___ ___ ___ ___ ___ M

Write the words.

month _____   number _____

Mrs. Norman _____

Write the sentence.

Mr. Nelson moved to Main Street.

Name Your Hobby

Stamps Sewing Painting Models Names Coins

Write three hobbies in each group.

THINGS YOU MAKE

1. _____

2. _____

3. _____

THINGS YOU COLLECT

1. _____

2. _____

3. _____

What is your favorite hobby?

_____

_____

_____

Trace and write the letters.

V V

V V

W W

W W

Write the words.

wolves _____   waves _____

West Virginia _____

Write the question.

Will you visit Val Wilson?

Where do you live?

Finish the sentences to tell where the children live.

William lives in

Elena

Vivian

Paul

Wisconsin · Vivian

Vermont · Paul

Virginia · William

Wyoming · Elena

Write the name of your city and state.

Trace and write the letters.

y Y

k K

Write the sentence.

A yak and a kiwi are animals.

Yak

Kiwi

Write the name of each animal.

46

Y Y k K

Yaks live in Tibet.

Kiwis live in New Zealand.

A yolla and a kenot are imaginary animals. Write the name of each animal.

Draw pictures of what you think the yolla and kenot look like.

Write where you think the yolla and kenot live.

Trace and write the letters.

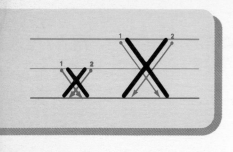

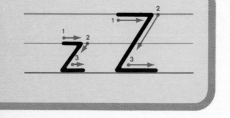

x X x x _ _ _ _ _ _ x

X X _ _ _ _ _ _ X

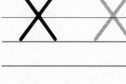

z Z z z _ _ _ _ _ _ z

Z Z _ _ _ _ _ _ Z

Write the words.

taxi _____

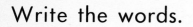

X-ray _____

zero _____

Zip Code _____

Write the sentence.

Zeke stacked the sixteen boxes.

The xylophone and the zither are musical instruments that are fun to play. Choose a silly sentence to write by each of the pictures.

xylophone **zither**

Zelda Zebra plays a zither. They clapped when Ollie Ox played the xylophone.

X and **Z** are letters that are fun to write and put in pictures.
Make your own pictures on drawing paper with **X** and **Z**.

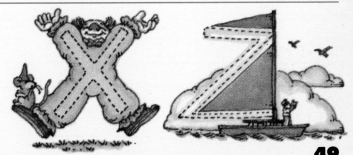

49

Write the missing numerals. Count by ones.

1   2   ___   4   ___

6   7   ___   9   ___

Count by fives.

5   10   15   ___   25   ___

35   40   45   ___   55   ___

65   70   75   ___   85   90

Count by tens.

10   ___   30   ___   50

60   ___   80   ___   100

110   120   ___   140   ___

50

Lisa, Mark, and Mei Ling are friends. They want to see who is the tallest. Look at the graph.

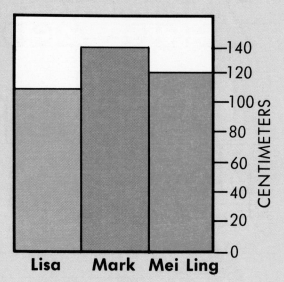

CENTIMETERS

Lisa   Mark   Mei Ling

Shortest and Tallest

Write a sentence to answer each question.

Who is the tallest?

_____

Who is the shortest?

_____

Who is taller, Lisa
or Mei Ling?

_____

Who is shorter,
Mark or Lisa?

_____

Write the children's names in order from the shortest to the tallest.

_____

_____

Measure your height in centimeters. Write how tall
you are.

Read these sentences. Write the one that tells
about you.

- • I am taller than Mark.
- • I am shorter than Lisa.
- • I am between Lisa and Mark.

_____

Write the sentences with correct punctuation.

The children meet to play soccer

_____

1. _____

_____

Pat shouts I will kick the ball

_____

2. _____

_____

Just then a dog runs on the field

_____

3. _____

_____

Look at what is happening

4.

What will the children do now

5.

Write what you think will happen next.

6.

My letter forms are:

CORRECT ☐

INCORRECT ☐

Lower-Case Letters

Write the lower-case letter for each letter below.

B_ H_ P_ R_ N_ M_

V_ W_ K_ Y_ X_ Z_

Write the names of things in the picture
that begin with the letters shown above.

Creative Thinking

Write sentences that tell about the picture.

My letters are the correct size.
YES ☐   **NO** ☐
My spacing is correct.
YES ☐   **NO** ☐

My brother

The kitten

A funny clown

**WHO
or
WHAT**

at the circus

on the sidewalk

by the door

WHERE

purrs loudly

did tricks

found a quarter

**WHAT
HAPPENED**

last night.

this morning.

when it is hungry.

WHEN

Choose one phrase from each group of cards to write
a sentence. Then finish writing your story.

_____

_____

_____

_____

_____

_____

_____

_____

_____

_____

_____

_____

_____

_____

Review the top-to-bottom stroke. Trace and write the strokes.

Underline ten different letters in your story that have top-to-bottom strokes.

What Needs Lines?

Complete the pictures with left-to-right lines.

Paper needs lines.
Telephone poles need lines.
Clothes need lines.

Write the three sentences.

1. _____

2. _____

3. _____

Musical Notes Need Lines

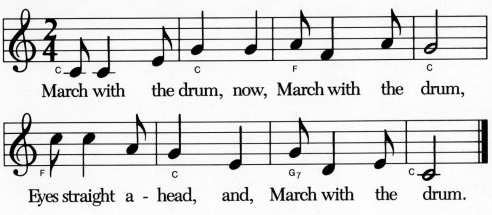

March with   the drum, now, March with   the drum,

Eyes straight a - head,   and, March with   the   drum.

March with the Drum

American Folk Tune

Write the words of the song.

 CHECK-UP

My left-to-right strokes are correct.

YES ☐   **NO** ☐

59

Backward Circle

Trace and write the backward circles. Write the letters.

O O   o o

a__ c__ d__ e__ g__ o__

q__ O__ C__ G__ Q__

Write the sentence.

Greg won first place.

Write a sentence to tell what kind of contest you think Greg won.

My backward circles are closed.

YES ☐   NO ☐

60

How many words can you write using these letters?

o c a e d l g i t

1. cold

2. _____

3. _____

4. _____

5. _____

6. _____

7. _____

8. _____

9. _____

10. _____

My backward circles are closed.
YES ☐   NO ☐

My letters are straight.
YES   NO ☐

Forward Circle

Trace and write the forward circle. Write the words.

O　　O　　— — — — —　　O

peppers _____

pebbles _____

Unscramble the letters to make words.

epbe _____

ubmp _____

pyupp _____

ocpropn _____

HOW TO HOLD YOUR PENCIL

Points toward left elbow

left-handed

Pencil near big knuckle

First finger on top

Bend thumb

Points toward right shoulder

right-handed

Last two fingers touch paper

Write the sentence telling what mistake these children are making.

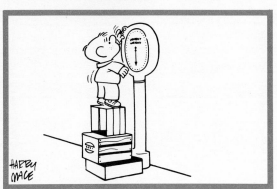

- The weight of the boxes will break the scale.
- The boxes will make the boy weigh more than he really does.

- The girl is tying the swing too low.
- The tree is too tall for the swing.

Slant Line Letters

Trace and write the slant lines.

In My Grandfather's Trunk I Found:

How many things can you find in this picture that have at least one slant line letter in their name?

1.

2.

3.

4.

5.

6.

7. _____

8. _____

9. _____

10. _____

11. _____

12. _____

13. _____

14. _____

15. _____

16. _____

17. _____

18. _____

65

Write the correct lower-case letters for each group.

⬇ **STRAIGHT LINE LETTERS**

↺ **BACKWARD CIRCLE LETTERS**

CURVE LINE LETTERS

✓ Which is your best group of letters?

straight line letters ☐
backward circle letters ☐
curve line letters ☐

⟳ FORWARD CIRCLE LETTERS

◣◤ SLANT LINE LETTERS

Write the tall lower-case letters.

Write the tail letters.

✓ Which is your best group of letters?
forward circle letters ☐
slant line letters ☐
tall letters ☐
tail letters ☐

Words with the Same Starters

hungry horse   creaky cricket   dancing dolphins
_____   _____   _____

musical mouse   singing swan   friendly frog

Choose four to write.
_____

1._____

2._____

3._____

4._____

Write two of your own. Begin
both words with the same letter.
_____

1._____

2._____

What would happen if...

lamps could laugh?
trees could trot?
cookies could cough?

windows could whisper?
sandwiches could smile?

Complete this sentence.

If lamps could laugh

Choose different groups of words from above to write two more sentences.

1.

2.

	CORRECT	INCORRECT
letter formation	☐	☐
line quality	☐	☐
spacing	☐	☐

Tongue Twisters

Say each tongue twister quickly three times.

> **Two tiny toads trotted to town.**
>
> **Five flies float from the flowers.**
>
> **Cookie cutters cut cute cookies.**
>
> **Billy Biggs bought brown bread.**

Write the tongue twister you like the best.

_____

_____

_____

_____

_____

Write a tongue twister of your own.

_____

_____

_____

_____

_____

_____

All my letters are the correct size.

YES ☐　　NO ☐

Days of the Week QUIZ

Sunday • Monday • Tuesday • Wednesday
Thursday • Friday • Saturday

Answer these questions with a day of the week.

1. What day comes before Thursday?
2. What is the first day of the week?
3. What day comes after Monday?
4. What is the last day of the school week?
5. What is the first day of the school week?

6. What day is Thanksgiving day?
7. What day have you not written?

4. _____

1. _____

2. _____

5. _____

6. _____

3. _____

7. _____

What is your favorite day of the week? Why?

_____

My letters are smooth.

YES ☐   NO ☐

STRAIGHT LINE LETTERS

L   I   T

E   F   H

CIRCLE LETTERS

O   C   G   Q

1. Which straight line letter has three slide right strokes?

1. _____

2. Which straight line letter has two top-to-bottom strokes?

2. _____

3. Which circle letter has a slant stroke?

3. _____

4. Which circle letter has a slide right stroke?

4. _____

5. Which four straight line letters require two lifts of the pencil?

5. _____

72

CURVE LINE LETTERS

R ___ U ___ S ___ D ___

B ___ P ___ J ___

SLANT LINE LETTERS

A ___ K ___ N ___ M ___

V ___ W ___ X ___ Y ___ Z ___

1. Which curve line letter has a slant stroke?

1. _____

2. Which curve line letters have slide right strokes?

2. _____

3. Which slant line letters have only one slant stroke?

3. _____

4. Which slant line letters have one top-to-bottom stroke?

4. _____

Number Puzzle

Fill in the puzzle with the number words from one to ten.
Use upper-case letters.

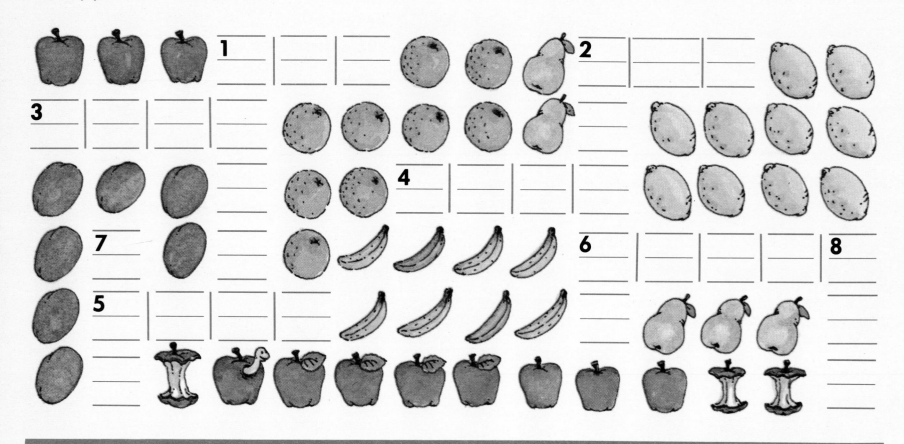

ACROSS

1. How many yellow bananas do you see?
2. How many bananas are green?
3. How many pears do you see?
4. How many apples have leaves?
5. How many oranges do you see?
6. How many bananas in all?

DOWN

1. How many plums do you see?
2. How many apples have been eaten?
7. How many apples have a worm?
8. How many lemons do you see?

Code

Look at the code.
Write the correct letters using your best upper-case manuscript writing.

What tree can you hold in your hand?

8 2 12 9

_____
_____
_____

What starts with a **T**, ends with a **T**, and is full of **T**?

4 7 2 8 10 4

_____
_____
_____

What six-letter word has a mile between each **s**?

3 9 11 12 7 3

_____
_____
_____

What vegetable do you get when you drop a pumpkin?

3 1 6 2 3 5

_____
_____
_____

75

1. Write the upper and lower-case straight line letters.

1.

2. Write the upper and lower-case backward circle letters.

2.

3. Write the upper and lower-case letters that have a left to right stroke.

3.

4. Write the upper and lower-case slant line letters.

4.

5. Write the lower-case forward circle letters.

5.

CHECK-UP

My letters are the correct size.

YES ☐   NO ☐

Compound Words: **words made by putting together two smaller words**

Draw a line to match two words that make a compound word.
Write the compound word.

1.	wind	bow
2.	rain	shoe
3.	air	fly
4.	horse	cakes
5.	butter	mill
6.	mail	plane
7.	snow	flake
8.	pan	box

Write three compound words of your own.

1. _____

2. _____

3. _____

1. _____

2. _____

3. _____

4. _____

5. _____

6. _____

7. _____

8. _____

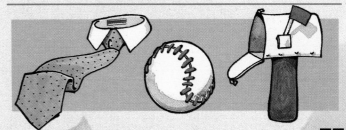

Tail Letters

Write each letter.

g   j   p   q   y

Which tail letter has a
forward circle in it?

Which tail letters have
backward circles in them?

Which tail letter is made
with slant strokes?

Write a word that begins with each tail letter.

g   j

p   q   y

Write the sentence. The dog jumped over the fence.

Missing Tails

These letters are missing tails. Complete each letter.

a i p a v

The monkey, bluejay, goat, pig, prairie dog, and quail are missing their tails. Write the name of each animal. Match the animal with its tail.

1. _____

2. _____

3. _____

4. _____

5. _____

6. _____

1. monkey

2. bluejay

3. goat

4. pig

5. prairie dog

6. quail

Rhyming Words

THE SKY

The sky is high; the sky is blue.
The sky is always looking at you.

KELLY BROWN, Age 7

Find a word in the cloud that rhymes with each word below. Write the rhyming word.

stop   wing   silk
rake   you   would
                  key
   table   wink
        club   room
                     drift

swift	rub	milk	could
able	drink	snake	broom
blue	shop	bee	thing

Write a sentence telling what you see when you look at the sky.

Writing Two-Line Poems

FLUFF | Kitty, kitty, drinking milk.
Your fur is fine and soft as silk.

FLOWERS | I like flowers red and blue.
Pink and yellow will suit me, too.

THE RIVER | The river is swift.
My boat will drift.

Choose one poem. Write it on these lines.

_____

_____

_____

_____

_____

Write a two-line poem of your own. The words at
the end of the line should rhyme.

_____

_____

_____

_____

_____

Circle four words or phrases that describe an owl. Write the words to complete the sentences.

| beak | fur | hunt at night |
| hooves | wise | build nests |

Emily was not ignorant. She was ____ .

_____

_____

_____

Many owls ____ in trees.

_____

_____

_____

The owl has a short ____ .

_____

_____

_____

Owls ____ for food.

_____

_____

_____

_____

An owl says, "Whoo-oo!" Write these sounds by the animals that make them.

| tweet • croak • grrrr • squeak |

82

Do you know why?

Write answers to these questions.

Why do squirrels gather acorns?

_____

_____

_____

_____

Why do birds collect grass and twigs?

_____

_____

_____

_____

Why do worms live underground?

_____

_____

_____

_____

Write one question you would like to ask about owls.

_____

_____

_____

_____

My spacing is correct.

YES ☐   NO ☐

83

SPACING BETWEEN WORDS

This•is•correct•spacing.

SPACING BETWEEN SENTENCES

Write the sentences.

I like summer.••Do you?

hot

sunshine

travel

fishing

swimming

backpack

garden

vacation

picnic

camping

barbecue

rain

Write about Summer

Use the words on page 84.

CHECK-UP

My spacing is correct.

YES ☐   NO ☐

Using the Dictionary

Think of a dictionary as having three parts.

The first part of the dictionary has words beginning with letters **A—F**. Choose three words you would find in the first part. Write the words in alphabetical order.

The middle part of the dictionary has words beginning with letters **G—P**. Choose three words you would find in the middle part. Write the words in alphabetical order.

The last part of the dictionary has words beginning with letters **Q—Z**. Choose three words you would find in the last part. Write the words in alphabetical order.

weather   even   thirty   rowboat   nickel

camel   lemon   dozen   jacket

FIRST

1. _____

2. _____

3. _____

MIDDLE

1. _____

2. _____

3. _____

LAST

1. _____

2. _____

3. _____

Write a sentence that tells how a dictionary helps you.

_____

_____

86

The words in a dictionary are in alphabetical order.
Write these words in alphabetical order.

joke

bowl

tires   kitchen   lunch

sandwich   puddle   house

1. _____
2. _____
3. _____
4. _____

5. _____
6. _____
7. _____
8. _____

Use the words in sentences of your own.

_____
_____
_____
_____
_____
_____

This is good alignment.

These are scrambled sentences.
Write the words in alphabetical order to unscramble the sentences.

1. climbed   tree   A   the   bear

2. plant   him   yams   Don   helped

3. my   by   window   Bees   buzzed

✓ CHECK-UP

All my letters rest on the baseline.	YES ☐	NO ☐
All my short letters touch the midline.	YES ☐	NO ☐
All my tall letters touch the headline.	YES ☐	NO ☐
All my tail letters fill the space below the baseline.	YES ☐	NO ☐

above   before   fix   buy   first   full
same   heavy   noisy   close   back   push   take
slow

Write a word that means the opposite of each word below.
Choose a word from the cloud.

last
_____
_____
_____
_____

open
_____
_____
_____
_____

front
_____
_____
_____
_____

give
_____
_____
_____
_____

quiet
_____
_____
_____
_____

below
_____
_____
_____
_____

break
_____
_____
_____
_____

empty
_____
_____
_____
_____

after
_____
_____
_____
_____

sell
_____
_____
_____
_____

pull
_____
_____
_____
_____

fast
_____
_____
_____
_____

different
_____
_____
_____
_____

light
_____
_____
_____
_____

CHECK-UP

The size of my writing is correct.

YES ☐   NO ☐

Write about Things You Like

I like the smell of cut grass.
I like the taste of peanut butter.

Write what you like. Start each sentence
with "I like. . . ."

feel

I like the feel of

taste

smell

Write about Wishes

I wish I could fly like a bird.
I wish I could climb a mountain.

Write your wishes.

I wish

I wish

I wish

I wish

My letters are smooth.

YES ☐   NO ☐

Sometimes two different words mean the same thing.

| The play is about to begin. • The play is about to start. |

The words **begin** and **start** mean the same thing.

Once there was an honest shoemaker. He worked hard to make enough money for his family. He stitched leather together to make shoes.

Find an underlined word in the story that means the same as each of these words. Write it in the space.

earn

sewed

fair

dollars

Sentences that mean the same

Choose the sentence that means the same as the first sentence. Write it.

The shoemaker lived in a cottage.
- The shoemaker lived in a small house.
- The shoemaker slept on a cot.

Every morning he awoke early to do his job.
- Every day he left home at noon.
- Each morning he got up early to work.

The shoemaker was a fair person.
- The shoemaker was honest.
- The shoemaker was very happy.

He could not make enough money.
- He had a lot of money.
- He was very poor.

Years ago, many schoolhouses were one-room log cabins. Students of all ages were taught by one teacher in the same room.

Write the sentences. Use your best writing.

_____

_____

_____

_____

_____

_____

_____

_____

_____

_____

CHECK-UP

	CORRECT	INCORRECT
letter formation	☐	☐
vertical quality	☐	☐
spacing	☐	☐
alignment and proportion	☐	☐
line quality	☐	☐

Student Record of Handwriting Skills

MANUSCRIPT

PAGE		NEEDS IMPROVEMENT	MASTERY OF SKILL
6	Writes the top-to-bottom stroke within letters and words.	☐	☐
6	Writes the left-to-right stroke.	☐	☐
6	Writes the slant-left stroke.	☐	☐
7	Writes the slant-right stroke.	☐	☐
7	Writes the backward circle.	☐	☐
7	Writes the forward circle.	☐	☐
8-9	Size and alignment are correct.	☐	☐
9	Writes the middle-size and tail (descender) letters.	☐	☐
10	Writes the numerals **1-10.**	☐	☐
12	Positions paper properly.	☐	☐
12	Vertical quality is correct.	☐	☐
13	Holds pencil properly.	☐	☐
13	Line quality is correct.	☐	☐
14	Spacing between letters is correct.	☐	☐
15	Spacing between words and sentences is correct.	☐	☐
18-19	Writes the letter **I.**	☐	☐
18-19	Writes the letter **L.**	☐	☐

PAGE		NEEDS IMPROVEMENT	MASTERY OF SKILL
18-19	Writes the letter **i.**	☐	☐
18-19	Writes the letter **l.**	☐	☐
20-21	Writes the letter **t.**	☐	☐
20-21	Writes the letter **T.**	☐	☐
22-23	Writes the letter **o.**	☐	☐
22-23	Writes the letter **O.**	☐	☐
22-23	Writes the letter **a.**	☐	☐
22-23	Writes the letter **A.**	☐	☐
24-25	Writes the letter **d.**	☐	☐
24-25	Writes the letter **D.**	☐	☐
24-25	Writes the letter **c.**	☐	☐
24-25	Writes the letter **C.**	☐	☐
24	Writes the question mark.	☐	☐
26-27	Writes the letter **e.**	☐	☐
26-27	Writes the letter **E.**	☐	☐
26-27	Writes the letter **f.**	☐	☐
26-27	Writes the letter **F.**	☐	☐
26-27	Writes the comma.	☐	☐
30-31	Writes the letter **g.**	☐	☐
30-31	Writes the letter **G.**	☐	☐
30-31	Writes the letter **j.**	☐	☐
30-31	Writes the letter **J.**	☐	☐
32-33	Writes the letter **q.**	☐	☐

PAGE		NEEDS IMPROVEMENT	MASTERY OF SKILL
32-33	Writes the letter **Q**.	☐	☐
32-33	Writes the letter **u**.	☐	☐
32-33	Writes the letter **U**.	☐	☐
32-33	Writes the exclamation mark.	☐	☐
34-35	Writes the letter **s**.	☐	☐
34-35	Writes the letter **S**.	☐	☐
38-39	Writes the letter **b**.	☐	☐
38-39	Writes the letter **B**.	☐	☐
38-39	Writes the letter **h**.	☐	☐
38-39	Writes the letter **H**.	☐	☐
38-39	Writes quotation marks.	☐	☐
40-41	Writes the letter **p**.	☐	☐
40-41	Writes the letter **P**.	☐	☐
40-41	Writes the letter **r**.	☐	☐
40-41	Writes the letter **R**.	☐	☐
42-43	Writes the letter **n**.	☐	☐
42-43	Writes the letter **N**.	☐	☐
42-43	Writes the letter **m**.	☐	☐

PAGE		NEEDS IMPROVEMENT	MASTERY OF SKILL
42-43	Writes the letter **M**.	☐	☐
44-45	Writes the letter **v**.	☐	☐
44-45	Writes the letter **V**.	☐	☐
44-45	Writes the letter **w**.	☐	☐
44-45	Writes the letter **W**.	☐	☐
46-47	Writes the letter **y**.	☐	☐
46-47	Writes the letter **Y**.	☐	☐
46-47	Writes the letter **k**.	☐	☐
46-47	Writes the letter **K**.	☐	☐
48-49	Writes the letter **x**.	☐	☐
48-49	Writes the letter **X**.	☐	☐
48-49	Writes the letter **z**.	☐	☐
48-49	Writes the letter **Z**.	☐	☐
72	Categorizes letters by stroke similarities.	☐	☐
76	Writes the upper and lower-case letters in groups according to basic strokes.	☐	☐

STUDENT'S NAME